IMAGES
of America
THE GRAND HOTELS
OF ST. LOUIS

To Connie,

Enjoy these memories of
St. Louis.

Dan Fuller

This drawing of the Lennox lobby is signed by the architect, Preston J. Bradshaw. (Courtesy of Judy Bradshaw Miller.)

IMAGES
of America

THE GRAND HOTELS
OF ST. LOUIS

Patricia Treacy

ARCADIA

Published by Arcadia Publishing
Charleston SC, Chicago IL, Portsmouth NH, San Francisco CA

Printed in Great Britain

Library of Congress Catalog Card Number: 2005928682

For all general information contact Arcadia Publishing at:
Telephone 843-853-2070
Fax 843-853-0044
E-mail sales@arcadiapublishing.com
For customer service and orders:
Toll-Free 1-888-313-2665

Visit us on the internet at http://www.arcadiapublishing.com

Grand hotels were our city's hubs of activity, beating in rhythm with the Roaring Twenties. They suffered hard times later in the 20th century and crumbled under the pressure. Their resurrections make them some of our city's best-loved treasures. These hotels are presented in the order in which they debuted, not according to their importance. Choosing the most important one is like being forced to name the favorite among your children. Each hotel holds a special memory for someone. Some of these remembrances are recorded in this book. (Courtesy of St. Louis Public Library, Special Collections.)

CONTENTS

FOREWORD

Historic hotels have lives all their own. A hotel's life often parallels human life. It has ups and downs, triumphs and tragedies.

This book takes you back in time to the early 20th century. St. Louis was the sixth largest city in the country and a regional trade center with 26 trains rumbling through a five-state area. Local boosters advertised the city as the "49th state."

It was the height of the Jazz Age. Flappers wore bobbed hair, short skirts, turn-down hose, and powdered knees to dance the Charleston.

St. Louis was ripe for luxury hotels, and five grand hotels were built between 1917 and 1929. Each of these hotels had its own personality, its own culture, and its own register of distinguished guests. This hotel building boom screeched to a halt when the stock market crashed. It would be more than 30 years before another new hotel would appear on the St. Louis downtown horizon.

The Jefferson Hotel is not included in this book because its public spaces are not readily available for the eye to see. The Jefferson opened for the 1904 World's Fair and has an illustrious history. It still stands and has been converted to apartments for the elderly under the name the New Jefferson Arms. The former nightclub, the Boulevard Room, can be rented for private parties, but the magnificent Gold Room has been closed for almost 30 years.

A remarkable fact is that the five grand hotels in this book have been restored and renewed and are as glamorous today as they were in their earlier days. These hotels seem to have nine lives. They survived the Great Depression, two world wars, and an exodus from the city. And their resurrections are as exciting as their births. They welcome you to enjoy their splendor.

Maybe you have visited these hotels in the past. You may have frolicked at an office party at the Mayfair dining room, or stopped for a snack at the Hofbrau after a movie. You may have had dinner at the popular Lennox Rathskeller or danced the night away in the two-story ballroom atop the Statler. Maybe you were thrilled by a famous entertainer at the Chase or stopped for a drink in the Coronado's Coal Hole. Or maybe you were a bride who crossed one of these hotels' thresholds. Whenever you passed the portals of these havens of hospitality, you were a special person.

Celebrated guests of today follow in the footsteps of those before them. One by one, each visitor adds to the hotels' legacies.

INTRODUCTION
St. Louis's Glorious Hotel History

St. Louis has been a proud leader in the hospitality business for more than two centuries. And the Gateway City did not come by its title as an "honorary" degree. St. Louis got the moniker the old-fashioned way: it earned it. Just as soon as the first wave of Easterners decided to reach the Land of Goshen way out west through the portal that St. Louis became, the city rose up to its obligation to be cordial and genial to all the pioneers, prospectors, planters, and profiteers who took up at least transitory residence in St. Louis.

As soon as the need arose to accommodate the wayfarers passing through St. Louis who could afford to sleep under a roof rather than under the stars, local taverners, rooming and boarding house operators, innkeepers, and hoteliers rose to the occasion of providing basic decent-to-luxurious lodgings.

Among St. Louis's most classic 19th century hotels were the National, the Southern, the Planter's House, and the Lindell.

The National Hotel opened in 1832 at Third and Market as St. Louis's finest hotel of its day. Room and board under the American plan cost a lodger $20 a month. Although it was built as a "honeymoon hotel," among its luminary guests were Daniel Webster and Jefferson Davis. The National was also the terminal for the first narrow gauge train that opened up St. Louis's suburbs.

The posh Southern, with its distinct Italianate architecture, was a favorite of such luminary patrons as Mark Twain. The great humorist had a quiver full of quips about the elegant hotel lounge's ancient billiard balls and cue sticks employed upon its 10 billiard tables. It is widely believed that Southern Comfort was first sipped at the Southern. Alas, the 350-room, palace-like hotel at Fourth and Walnut was wiped out by fire in the spring of 1877, rebuilt in 1881, closed in 1912, and totally erased from the horizon in 1933 after serving several other functions.

One of the distinctions of the grand old Planter's Hotel with its 300 guest rooms is that it made not one, but three debuts—the first was in 1817, the second was by restoration in 1841, and the third was at Fourth and Chestnut in 1892. The building was heavily damaged by fire in 1887, torn down and rebuilt in 1891 with an additional 100 rooms. During the glory days of the Planters' House, wealthy cotton and tobacco plantation owners often brought their entire families and a cadre of slaves and servants to spend the season—the entire winter—there. Were it around today, the plush old hotel could feature wall plaques that quite accurately boasted that Presidents Van Buren, Lincoln, and Grant, Civil War hero William Tecumseh Sherman, and Charles Dickens slept there. The famous cocktail, the Tom Collins, was first concocted there. Whether or not Planter's Punch was created there is a matter of debate. Planters' House was turned into an office building in 1922, and the structure was razed in 1933.

Among the Lindell Hotel's unique amenities in the late 1870s were steam heat and lace curtains in every room and a massage bath powered by electricity. And Lindell Hotel patrons had their choice of cold water, Russian, or Turkish baths. The hotel barbershop featured a dozen premier barbers whose customers were served in leather-upholstered chairs. And tonsorial services at the Lindell served more than its resident and transient guests. One of those barbers operating out of the Lindell grossed a reported $2,000 a month (in 1870s dollars) and claimed 600 regular customers from all over St. Louis.

Unfortunately these classic St. Louis hotels of yesteryear were lost forever due to fires, neglect, economic downturns, and pure reckless wrecking. But thank goodness, all is not lost for those of us who can appreciate the grand style, high ceilings, opulent fixtures, classic furnishings, pampering, and regal service in the tradition of the grand old hotels. You are about to read about five venerable St. Louis hotels that managed to survive the headache ball and even those spectacular implosions to experience glorious rebirth. Ready to check in? Your room is ready!

—Julius K. Hunter

Julius K. Hunter, an award-winning author, historian, educator, lecturer, and 33-year veteran reporter/anchor of St. Louis broadcast news, is currently vice president for community relations at St. Louis University.

This plaque hangs on the outside wall of the Lennox Hotel facing Washington Avenue. (Photograph by Gene Donaldson.)

One

THE STATLER

Now the Renaissance Grand Hotel on Washington Avenue at Eighth Street, the Statler was listed on the National Register of Historic Places on March 19, 1982. (Courtesy of the Missouri Historical Society, St. Louis; photograph by W. C. Persons, 1928.)

When Ellsworth M. Statler chose St. Louis as the site for his fourth hotel, local citizens were jubilant. His architectural masterpiece put St. Louis on the modern hotel map.

The Statler was not Ellsworth's first major project in St. Louis. David R. Francis, president of the Louisiana Purchase Exposition to be held in St. Louis in 1904, wired the hotel man, then residing in Buffalo, New York, about building a temporary hotel inside the fairgrounds. The result was Statler's Inside Inn, a grand hotel topped with two Moorish towers with 2,257 rooms, 500 baths, and two dining rooms that seated 2,000 people each. When waiters performed unsatisfactorily, he replaced them with 287 women, a first in the industry. He hired 1,000 employees to run the Inside Inn.

In 1908, he built his first permanent luxury hotel in Buffalo, New York, insisting that each room have its own bath, another first. Statler advised the architect to place pipes for adjoining rooms back-to-back and stack the bathrooms so that each set on one floor was directly below those above. This system is still used today and in architectural schools it is known as the "Statler plumbing shaft." The hotel man advertised his new hotel as "a room and a bath for a dollar and a half." Hotels in Cleveland and Detroit were next. When he ventured into St. Louis, he left a lasting mark on the city.

St. Louis society welcomed the Statler's lavish public rooms for high teas and the stunning rooftop ballroom for dinner dances. Then-senator Harry S. Truman and Republican presidential candidates Wendell L. Willkie, Alf Landon, and Tom Dewey stayed at the Statler. Both legendary wrestler Ed (Strangler) Lewis, and boxer Benny Leonard, made the Statler their homes away from home.

Statler chose a site on the eastern edge of the wholesale district at Ninth Street and Washington Avenue, just north of the new Orpheum Theater. He hired renowned George B. Post and Sons of New York, who had designed his Detroit and Cleveland hotels, to draw plans for the lavish structure.

The 650-room, 20-story hotel cost $3 million to build, although promoters said it would have cost $4 million if Statler had not stockpiled structural steel and furnishings two years in advance. It was a model of elegance.

The St. Louis Art League celebrated the new hotel as a work of "pre-eminent artistic merit," and *Hotel World* called it "Statler's public palace."

The Statler opened in 1917, the year jazz singer Ella Fitzgerald and poet T. S. Eliot were born. Pres. Woodrow Wilson sent U.S. troops to Europe to fight in World War I, and patriotic Americans bought liberty bonds. But the excitement in St. Louis was the opening of the Statler Hotel.

The Hospital Saturday and Sunday Association fête on November 9 let 1,500 people preview the hotel before its opening the next day. Guests in sparkling jewels paid $7.50 to attend the charity reception. Statler also hosted a dinner for newspaper publishers and editors.

A capacity crowd of 1,600 people, all of whom reserved dinner at $3.50 a plate, filled the hotel the next evening, and hundreds more were turned away. Dinner was served in relays in the hotel's six dining rooms. Three orchestras played throughout the hotel as guests toured the nine acres of floor space. Newspaper accounts of the opening noted that women were permitted to smoke in the public dining room, a new Statler innovation.

Guests marveled at elevator girls piloting the four passenger elevators, usually run by men. Visitors commented about the lending library of 1,500 books and circulating ice water in every room, a Statler trademark.

Statler distributed copies of his 17-page Statler Service Code to his 500 employees. His code guaranteed satisfaction to every guest. The hotel man coined the phrase: "The guest is always right."

Ellsworth M. Statler is dubbed "America's Extraordinary Hotelman" by biographer Floyd Miller. He was one of nine children, born into poverty in 1863 in Pennsylvania. At age nine, Statler quit school in the third grade to haul coal and fire a furnace in a glassworks factory. He began his hotel career as a bellboy at McClure House, an imposing five-story hotel in Wheeling, West Virginia. He earned $6 a month. By 16, he had taught himself to handle the hotel's books and at 19 was the untitled manager. In 1894, he moved to Buffalo, New York, where "the biggest office building in the world" was under construction, to open a restaurant in the building. When plans for Buffalo's Pan-American Exposition were announced, Statler built "the world's largest hotel" next to the fairgrounds, a temporary wood structure to be demolished at the end of the fair. (Courtesy of the Statler Foundation, Buffalo, New York.)

Statler hired George B. Post and Sons of New York City to design his masterpiece. This is the architect's drawing of the 20-story hotel. (Courtesy of Historic Restoration, Inc., Properties.)

This photograph shows the detail of the lower floors of the Statler. The exterior up to the fifth floor was finished in buff Bedford limestone. Overhanging balconies of limestone highlighted the 16th floor and the remaining top floors were of glazed terra cotta. (Courtesy of Historic Restoration, Inc., Properties.)

Step into one of the Statler dining rooms. Doors opened to the outside for ventilation. The Palm Room, another public dining room, was in the center of the mezzanine. It was bedecked in palms, flowers in gaily painted boxes, and a cream-and-green marble floor. (Courtesy of the Missouri Historical Society, St. Louis; photograph by W. C. Persons, 1928.)

This shows the elaborate service screen in the center dining room. Waiters moved in and out of this area to serve their 400 guests. The main dining room had a steel and milk glass skylight that was replicated during the restoration. (Courtesy of the St. Louis Public Library, Fine Arts Department.)

Menu covers were works of art in the hotel's early days. Here are two samples. (Courtesy of St. Louis Public Library, Special Collections.)

This menu listed the a la carte items.

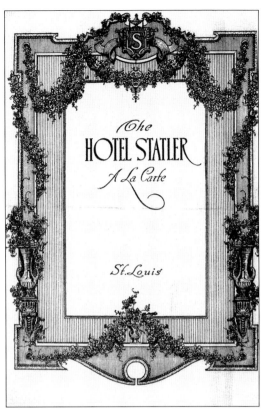

The 1926 New Year's Day menu cover showed "1925" in the bottom of the hourglass. (Courtesy of St. Louis Public Library, Special Collections.)

This early postcard gave a history lesson on the back: "St. Louis is modern in fine hotels, office buildings, beautiful parks, and has many of the finest homes in the country, and at the same time is older than the U.S. and rich in romantic tradition. Three flags floated over St. Louis in one day in March 1803, when Spain ceded Louisiana back to France and France gave way to America." (Courtesy of St. Louis Public Library, Special Collections.)

The highlight of the hotel was the breathtaking two-story roof garden-ballroom that spanned the building with a 5,000-square-foot dance floor and stage. The windows, 22 feet high and 9 feet wide, opened to the floor with no sills. The ceiling was a vault painted in atmospheric tones of blue, simulating the sky. The roof garden had a colonnade of fluted piers topped by Corinthian capitals. During the summer, billowing ceilings of striped, bright-red tenting gave guests the out-of-doors feeling of the room. A narrow walkway above the ballroom gave security personnel bird's-eye surveillance of the entire room. High society in St. Louis found a home in the Statler ballroom overlooking the Mississippi River and the city. (Courtesy of Historic Restoration, Inc., Properties.)

The Statler was the backdrop for an historic event when the National American Suffrage Association held its golden jubilee convention at the hotel in March 1919. At that time, some states allowed women to vote only in presidential elections and some states did not allow women to vote at all. (The 19th Amendment to the Missouri Constitution, allowing women to vote, was finally passed in 1921.) Six hundred delegates from all states traveled to St. Louis for the five-day convention. It was described by the *St. Louis Post-Dispatch* as a meeting of "friendly intercourse and social splendor. The formal dinner was the most elaborate a scale in St. Louis in several years." The convention included afternoon teas from 3:00 to 5:00 p.m., special dinners for $1.50 per plate, and supper dances every evening at 11:00 p.m. The highlight of the convention was the creation of the League of Women Voters, formed to secure final political enfranchisement of women in every state. The Equal Suffrage League of St. Louis evolved into the League of Women Voters that still exists today. (Courtesy of Missouri Historical Society, St. Louis.)

In 1948, the Statler roof was the scene of University City High School's annual coronation ball. Pictured here are Gloria Gluskoter, sorority queen finalist, and her escort, Sel Polsky. (Courtesy of Gloria Golbart-Marks.)

This early advertisement touted the hotel. During the 1920s, afternoon tea with a special menu cost 50¢. Bill Walsh, a bellboy, worked at the Statler from 1920 to the 1950s. True to the Statler Service Code, Walsh learned who the guests were from the room clerk and addressed them by name. Most guests tipped him, usually a quarter, although he remembered a $5 tip. Walsh escorted Gen. John J. Pershing to his room when he came to St. Louis to dedicate Pershing School. (Courtesy of St. Louis Public Library, Special Collections.)

Statler's wife died in 1925 and two years later, he married Alice Seidler, his secretary. He died of pneumonia in 1928, the same year France conferred on Statler the cross of the Legion of Honor "in reward of his great service to mankind." His 45-year-old widow took over his hotels valued at $30 million, the richest corporation in the world controlled by a woman. Alice Statler ran the business for the next 26 years, opened additional hotels, and more than doubled the value of the enterprise. (Courtesy of the Statler Foundation, Buffalo, New York.)

Conrad Hilton paid $111 million to purchase the Statler chain from Alice Statler in 1954. This was the largest real estate transaction in American history up to that time. Hilton was born in San Antonio, New Mexico, in 1887, educated at St. Michael's College in Santa Fe, the New Mexico Military Institute, and the New Mexico School of Mines. He served a term in the first New Mexico state legislature before enlisting as a second lieutenant in World War I. After the war, the entrepreneur traveled to Texas where oil gushed, intending to buy a local bank. Instead he bought a rundown hotel, the Mobley, and rented rooms in eight-hour shifts to oil field workers. He built his first hotel in Dallas in 1925, the same year the 38-year-old hotel man married Mary Barron. They had three sons before they divorced in 1934. Hilton then married Zsa Zsa Gabor, and a daughter was born of this union before the couple divorced. On his 89th birthday in 1977, he married Mary Frances Kelly, whom he had known since the opening of the El Paso Hilton in 1930. In the 1940s, he bought the ailing Plaza Hotel and Waldorf-Astoria in New York and changed their red ink to black. He constructed his first hotel outside of the continental U.S. in San Juan, Puerto Rico, in 1949. Hilton built the largest hotel empire of his time and established the first American international hotel company. He was chairman of the corporation until his death in 1979. (Courtesy of the Hospitality Industry Archives, University of Houston.)

HILTON HOTELS

lead the way in fine dining . . .

Terrace
PRIME RIB ROOM

Now, as never before, during the evening dinner hour Hot Prime Rib of Beef will be carved and served directly from our Chef's Rib Wagon.

McCormick and Wray — St. Louis' most popular Piano-Organ Team entertain with delightful music.

THE STATLER BEEF STORY
Only the finest beef is served in the Rib Room. All beef purchases are carefully made by our Executive Chef. After 21 days of natural ageing under temperature and humidity control, this fine meat is ready for you. These are standard Statler processes and they are conducted with an extreme awareness that nothing but the finest is to be served to a Statler guest.

THE
STATLER
St. Louis' only Hilton Hotel

Ninth & Washington

Phone CEntral 1-1400

ask for Head Waiter Jerry Bush

Hilton retained the Statler name for the hotel, listing it as "St. Louis's only Hilton Hotel" in this advertisement. This advertisement also extols the quality of the hotel's beef. (Courtesy of St. Louis Public Library, Special Collections.)

The Statler was the favored destination for many corporate events. This photograph shows Shapleigh Hardware Company's 1956 salesmen's awards dinner at the Statler. King, Prince, and Big Chief of Divisions awards were presented by A. Lee Shapleigh II. The king and prince received diamond rings, and the big chiefs wore diamond lapel buttons. Long-term salesmen were also recognized. Former kings and princes from 1940 to the date of the banquet were listed in the program. The event was called the Keen Kutter banquet, and 75 salesmen attended. Keen Kutter was one of Shapleigh's brands of hardware. (Courtesy of Diane Edleson May.)

In 1966, Towne Realty Company of Milwaukee purchased the Statler and renamed it the St. Louis Gateway Hotel. By this time, downtown had lost its sparkle. In the mid-1970s, when Fred Cords was manager, he found "so-called ladies of the street pursuing their business in the hotel and pimps on staff." He cleaned up the hotel and opened it to railroad, barge, and trucking company employees under contract. In 1981, Victor Sayyah, a Denver businessman, and Peter J. Webbe, a St. Louis politician, bought the Gateway for $3.2 million and attempted a restoration. This photograph shows Bob Daniels of St. Louis stripping paint from one of the 18 large windows in 1984. (Courtesy of Suburban Journals; photograph by Rick Graefe.)

The Gateway closed in 1986 for renovation, and the once busy lobby was silent. In 1987, a fire raged through the building. Five firefighters suffered smoke inhalation in the blaze that took a day and a half to control. This photograph shows the windows facing Washington Avenue as they look today. (Photograph by Gene Donaldson.)

This photograph shows replacement of broken cornice work outside the two-story ballroom. After several years of complex public/private financing spearheaded by Historic Restoration, Inc., of New Orleans, work began to restore the original building and connect a new 23-floor hotel tower to the east. The $265 million project took three years to complete, and the hotel was renamed the Renaissance Grand Hotel. (Courtesy of *St. Louis Construction News*; photograph by Peter Downs.)

Restoration work on the ornate lobby and mezzanine was a challenge, as this photograph illustrates. Returning it to its original look is a tribute to the restoration architects, contractors, and artisans who accomplished the feat. (Courtesy of *St. Louis Construction News*; photograph by Peter Downs.)

This shows the atrium area under restoration. The original design of the room was recreated including the glass ceiling. (Courtesy of Historic Restoration, Inc., Properties.)

This is the atrium as it looks today. (Photograph by Alise O'Brien.)

This is the new Renaissance Grand bar, in the same location as the old Statler bar, stretching along Washington Avenue. During the Statler heyday, an organ and piano duo was popular entertainment in the bar. (Photograph by Alise O'Brien.)

This metal art, lighted from behind, is one of two that adorn the lounge area between the bar and the atrium. (Photograph by Gene Donaldson.)

This was the ballroom in July 1999 before restoration work began. (Courtesy of Historic Restoration Inc., Properties.)

This is the restored ballroom as it looks today. It has been renamed the Crystal Ballroom. (Photograph by Alise O'Brien.)

Kristen Poplstein was a bride in June 2003, shortly after the Renaissance Grand Hotel opened. Here she peers through one of the ballroom windows that meets the marble floor. (Photograph by Nordmann Photography.)

The bride and her father glide across the dance floor in the Crystal Ballroom. (Photograph by Nordmann Photography.)

The former Statler lobby is now An American Place, a fine restaurant. The ornate ceiling and columns have been meticulously restored. During the Statler era, the lobby opened to Washington Avenue on the north end and to St. Charles Street on the south end along Ninth Street. Today the entrance to the hotel is on Eighth Street. The entrance to the restaurant is on Washington Avenue at Ninth Street. (Photograph by Alise O'Brien.)

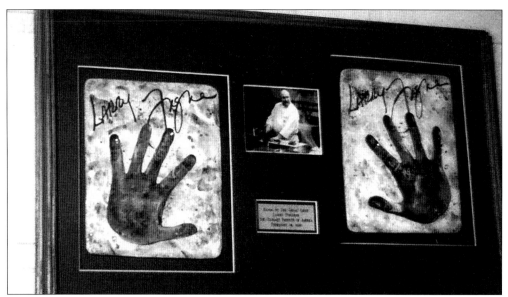

Larry Forgione's handprints hang on the wall of An American Place, his first restaurant outside of New York. His specialty is the use of raw products grown by local producers and farmers. (Photograph by Gene Donaldson.)

This three-dimensional artwork by William Lobdell hangs on the east restaurant wall, depicting the old Statler lobby. The artwork ties together the old and the new. This is still the place where business deals develop, romance blossoms, and families celebrate, as it has been since 1917. (Photograph by Gene Donaldson.)

Two

THE CHASE

Now the Chase-Park Plaza at Lindell and Kingshighway Avenues, the Chase was declared a city landmark in June 1977 and received Landmark Historic Status in 1982. (Courtesy of Landmarks Association of St. Louis; photograph by J. A. Bryan for *Missouri's Contribution to American Architecture*, 1928.)

The toastmaster of the grand opening on September 29, 1922, hailed the Chase Hotel as the "miracle of the miracle city." The guests at the gala event danced to music provided by Paul Whiteman's Pavilion Royale Orchestra of New York, a prelude to the hundreds of famed entertainers who would perform at the hotel through the years.

The Chase was a homegrown product that achieved national fame. It was built by a group of local investors headed by Chase Ulman, an attorney who owned two Lindell Avenue apartment buildings. The Chase is named for its builder. Even the furnishings were "made in St. Louis," provided by Stix, Baer and Fuller Department Store (now Dillard's).

The old *St. Louis Star-Times* newspaper reported, "In the words of a visiting hotel man, New York has been brought to St. Louis, but has been improved on."

But the dark cloud of the Great Depression loomed, and the hotel's future was threatened almost before it began. It changed hands seven times in its first nine years and slipped into bankruptcy in March 1931.

In the meantime, Sam Koplar built the Park Plaza Hotel, an art deco masterpiece adjacent to the Chase. The stock market crash of 1929 hit before the hotel was completed. The insurance company that then owned the Chase hired Koplar as desk clerk. He later became manager of the Chase Hotel and began buying the beleaguered hotel's stock. By 1947, he and his family owned 93.4 percent of the hotel and raised it to stardom. He retrieved the Park Plaza and joined it to the Chase in 1961. The duo became known as the Chase-Park Plaza Hotel.

"The Chase was the Mecca for everything in St. Louis—where the elite used to meet to eat and cheat," said the late Jack Buck, longtime St. Louis Cardinals announcer. "There was a lot of lobby-watching."

One memorable guest was a snake charmer who let her pets loose. But nothing was too much for employees at the Chase. Marilyn Krull, a longtime employee whose hand was kissed by Paul Anka, remembered the hotel's Braille menus and elevator signs for a national convention of 1,400 blind persons in 1981. A year later, the hotel was the host of the National Association of the Deaf convention and, in 1983, it was headquarters for the Miss Universe Pageant.

Ballet artist Rudolph Nureyev demanded a room with sunlight, and comedian Jack Benny simply said, "Just stick me anywhere."

The popular Zodiac Room had a large circular bar with the 12 signs of the Zodiac etched in the glass top. A silver figure of a girl with her head tilted to the sky was sculpted by Carl Mose, a Washington University professor. The figure sat on a pedestal in the center of the bar. Above her, a sliding dome could be opened to the outside. The unusual bar was sold at auction in the 1990s.

When the Starlight Roof opened, 7,000 young girls applied to carry cigarette trays, according to Analiese Von Frieling Stecher, who was a cigarette girl from 1940 to 1942. She was 16 years old in 1940 and earned $500 over the next two years to make a down payment on a house in Velda Village, in north St. Louis.

The stories and the stars of the Chase continue.

The Chase was built on the site of the William Bixby mansion and carriage house, with the hotel's entrance facing Lindell Boulevard. The reinforced concrete construction, performed by a local company, took only nine months for the nine-story, 500-room hotel designed by Preston J. Bradshaw. This construction photograph was taken on January 20, 1922. (Courtesy of the Missouri Historical Society, St. Louis.)

This is a close view of the ornate lower floors of the Chase. (Courtesy of the St. Louis Public Library, Fine Arts Department.)

These are some early interior pictures of the hotel. In keeping with its Italian Renaissance exterior design, much of the interior was elegantly furnished in that style. In 1927, a civic banquet was given for Charles A. Lindbergh at the Chase after his triumphant return to St. Louis. (Courtesy of the St. Louis Public Library, Fine Arts Department.)

These steps led to a large lounge area on the first floor. In later years, the Chase Club was adjacent to this area. Meanwhile, on the 17th floor, former presidents Dwight D. Eisenhower, Harry S. Truman, Jimmy Carter, Richard M. Nixon, John F. Kennedy, and Ronald Reagan were guests in the Chase's two-story presidential suite. Former vice presidents Spiro Agnew, Hubert H. Humphrey, and George W. Bush, as well as the Shah of Iran, also slept there. The suite had crystal chandeliers, a fireplace, 20-foot ceilings, and a spiral staircase leading to upstairs bedrooms. In 1978, the presidential suite cost $600 a day. (Courtesy of Judy Bradshaw Miller.)

This is an interior view of the hotel from 1922. (Courtesy of St. Louis Public Library, Fine Arts Department.)

This private dining room was in Italian style. The arched ceiling is elaborately decorated. (Courtesy of Judy Bradshaw Miller.)

This shows the intricate detail of the lounge area of the Chase. (Courtesy of St. Louis Public Library, Fine Arts Department.)

This public dining room was called the Palm Room. (Courtesy of Judy Bradshaw Miller.)

This was the main dining room in the Chase during the 1920s. A distinctive feature of the hotel was its series of dining rooms, each of a different period. One was in Italian, one in American Colonial design. The English-style dining room had wood paneled walls and brocade draperies, typical of the 1920s. Twin Waterford crystal chandeliers brought to the Chase from London were wired for electricity and hung in one of the dining rooms. (Courtesy of Judy Bradshaw Miller.)

This picture shows the Park Plaza towering above the Chase. Sam Koplar, who had made his fortune in the construction and operation of apartments, houses, hotels, and theaters, envisioned an art deco hotel next to the Chase after visiting New York's Savoy-Plaza. Construction began in 1929 on the shimmering silver-gray brick building with terra cotta trim. The 28-story structure rising 310 feet was built at a then-staggering cost of $6 million. He named it the Park Plaza: Park for Forest Park and Plaza for the Savoy-Plaza. While the hotel was under construction, the stock market crashed and Koplar lost control of his project. The Park Plaza was finally completed in 1930, and Koplar later gained ownership of both hotels. In 1961, Sam Koplar died, and his son, Harold, assumed leadership of the family business. At that time, the two hotels were combined and renamed the Chase-Park Plaza. (Courtesy of St. Louis Public Library, Fine Arts Department.)

John Davidson and his future bride, Harriett, both 19 years old, had dinner at the Chase Hotel on Thanksgiving Eve, November 27, 1946. It was the night before his draft notice ordered him to Seattle, Washington, to board a liberty ship bound for Japan with the U.S. Army of Occupation. "Liberty ships were built by Henry Kaiser in less than 30 days," explained Davidson. The three-year pre-medical student at Washington University worked night call in the ship's hospital. In 1960, the couple and their four children lived in the Central West End and had a $300 family membership at the Chase swimming pool. "One night we went to a luau at the pool, complete with hula dancers, a steel kettle drum band, tiki torches, and the limbo," they remembered. (Courtesy of John Davidson, M.D., and Mrs. Davidson.)

In December 1940, the open-air roof garden of the Chase was enclosed in glass, and the Starlight Roof and the adjoining Zodiac Room opened. This photo, from about 1950, shows Gloria Gluskoter dancing with Max Blinder, now a child psychologist, in the Zodiac Room. Comedian Sammy Shore stands on stage watching the dancers. On Tuesday evenings, the Zodiac Room awarded the best dancer a bottle of champagne. After accumulating many bottles of the bubbly wine, Gluskoter began teaching ballroom dancing at the Fred Astaire Studio in the Park Plaza. (Courtesy of Gloria Golbart-Marks.)

This family dinner in the Chase Club celebrated the 1949 high school graduation of Gloria Gluskoter, second from the right. (Courtesy of Gloria Golbart-Marks.)

Buddy Moreno's 14-piece orchestra was one of the local house bands playing in the Chase Club, beginning in 1947. Moreno is standing on the left side of the picture. The Chase Club closed in 1961, a victim of people's fascination with television and the skyrocketing cost of bringing name stars to St. Louis. Before it closed, Saturday afternoon tea dances and assembly dances for students of Mary Institute, John Burroughs, and Chaminade High School were held in the Chase Club. The dress code included white gloves. (Courtesy of Buddy Moreno.)

Entertainers, patrons, and employees all echoed, "the Chase is the Place," during the late 1940s and into the 1960s, when Las Vegas and New York celebrities beat a path to the Midwest to appear at the Chase Club. Dean Martin and Jerry Lewis played to a Chase Club audience of more than 1,600 customers in one of their first public appearances around 1950. Here Perry Como plants a kiss on a fan's cheek. The following pages show some of the many performers who appeared at the Chase Club. (Courtesy of George Cassimates, a maitre d' at the Chase from 1950 to 1977.)

Beatrice Kay, pictured here, was the "Gay Nineties Girl of Radio." (Courtesy of George Cassimates.)

Xavier Cugat, "the Rhumba King," opened at the Waldorf-Astoria Hotel in New York before playing at the Chase. (Courtesy of George Cassimates.)

Abbe Lane, vocalist with Xavier Cugat's orchestra, became one of the band leader's four wives. (Courtesy of George Cassimates.)

Singer Robert Goulet (left) and actress Carol Lawrence are pictured with George Cassimates. (Courtesy of George Cassimates.)

Eydie Gorme was a vocalist. (Courtesy of George Cassimates.)

Bob Hope signs autographs in the Chase lobby. (Courtesy of George Cassimates.)

Carmen Miranda was another popular singer to perform at the Chase. (Courtesy of George Cassimates.)

Sophie Tucker was "the last of the Red Hot Mamas." (Courtesy of George Cassimates.)

Spike Jones, zany band leader, was another Chase favorite. (Courtesy of George Cassimates.)

The Rat Pack, from left to right, Dean Martin, Johnny Carson (substituting for Joey Bishop), Frank Sinatra, and Sammy Davis Jr., entertained at Kiel Opera House to benefit Dismas House and stayed at the Chase. (Courtesy of George Cassimates.)

The publicity notice with Hildegarde's photograph read, "Milwaukee's international 'chantootsie' has just returned from Europe where she entertained American GIs on a U.S.O. tour of Army bases in Germany, Austria and Italy." (Courtesy of George Cassimates.)

Evelyn Knight was another marquee singer during the heyday of the Chase. (Courtesy of George Cassimates.)

Pictured here is the Mary Kaye Trio. (Courtesy of George Cassimates.)

Ray Anthony was a popular band leader. (Courtesy of George Cassimates.)

Josephine Baker, the famous singer, also appeared at the Chase. (Courtesy of George Cassimates.)

Pictured here are the Ted Lewis Dancers. (Courtesy of George Cassimates.)

Clyde McCoy appeared with his Sugar Blues Orchestra. (Courtesy of George Cassimates.)

Balladeer Nat "King" Cole always packed the house. (Courtesy of George Cassimates.)

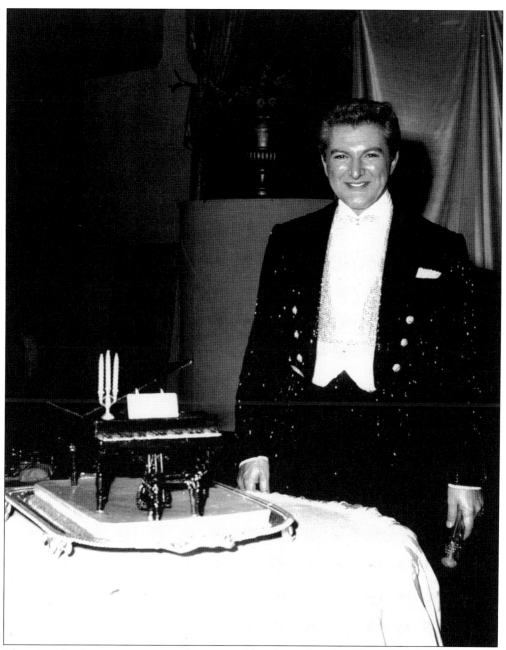

The piano in this picture was a cake prepared by the chef at the Chase for Liberace when he performed at the hotel. (Courtesy of George Cassimates.)

The spotlight in the world of sports fell on Stan "the Man" Musial during his testimonial dinner given by the St. Louis chapter of the Baseball Writers' Association at the Khorassan Room on October 20, 1963, the year he retired from playing for the St. Louis Cardinals. The cover of the program showed Amadee Wohlschlaeger's drawing of Stan signing an autograph for a boy, the statue that was later erected at Busch Stadium. The photograph shows the future Hall of Fame honoree with George Cassimates. (Courtesy of George Cassimates.)

These June 1952 graduates from Southwest High School celebrated the milestone at the Chase. The girls ensured their wrist corsages showed in the picture taken by the Chase photographer. (Courtesy of Joan Fiebelman, second from the right.)

Harry Fender was as colorful as the hotel itself. Here he interviews Guy Lombardo, left. Fender interviewed stars of screen and stage and everyone of importance who stopped by the Steeplechase Bar, now the Eau Bistro Restaurant. He broadcasted seven nights a week. Thelma Broderson, Fender's longtime friend, booked guests for the show in its later years. One unusual guest was a grizzly bear cub from the St. Louis Zoo. "Harry was fond of this cub and visited him every day. The cub even got to the point where he would take food from Harry's hand," Broderson recalled. "So, for Father's Day, I booked the cub for the show as a surprise for Harry. Two zookeepers brought him to the Chase and we hid him in the ladies room with a bucket of snow cones until it was time to go on the air," she said. When the entourage entered the Steeplechase, the bear growled over KMOX Radio. "The zoo named the cub Harry," Broderson added.

Harry Fender's mother was a dancer, and young Harry performed in local theater. He later starred in the Zeigfield Follies in New York before coming to St. Louis to walk a beat in the Central West End as a St. Louis police officer for 14 years. In 1959, when the Koplar family, owner of the Chase, was granted a license from the Federal Communications Commission for a new independent television station, KPLR-Channel 11 was born. In 1967, the Variety Club raised $176,000 during its 20-hour telethon on KPLR-TV. Sometimes the station did its newscast from the pool, with the announcer floating in an innertube while speaking into a microphone suspended from a bamboo pole. Harry Fender, well-known from his radio shows, became the headliner of "Captain 11's Showboat." In his Mark Twain–like wig and flowing mustache, Captain 11 entertained children in the studio audience and those at home. Fender died in 1995 at age 98. (Courtesy of the St. Louis Public Library Media Archives, Special Collections.)

Henry "Hack" Ulrich was on the cover of this Chase-Park Plaza publication, printed in the hotel's print shop. Hack Ulrich was another Chase legend, given the title of our "city's No. 1 host" by Ron Elz in his August 21, 1984 *St. Louis Globe-Democrat* column. Ulrich started working at the Chase as a busboy in 1935 and stayed for 50 years, becoming maitre d' of the Chase Club and the Tenderloin Room. "Anybody important who came into town, that's where they stayed—movie stars, politicians, sports figures, all of them. It was like New York City downtown every night. Everybody who played Las Vegas was there. It was wonderful. I loved going to work every day," Ulrich said in a 1998 interview. (Courtesy of the St. Louis Public Library, Special Collections.)

If you needed a table, you called Hack Ulrich. The Tenderloin Room opened in 1962, and 20 years later, it was renamed "Hack's Tenderloin Room" in honor of its popular host. Other than his years at the Chase, Ulrich had only two other jobs. His first job was a pitcher with the Cardinals Class B team in Lynchburg, Virginia, with teammate Red Schoendienst. His second appointment was a two-year stint in the army. Ulrich never returned to baseball, but instead began a long and successful career with the Chase, brushing elbows with show business personalities and important local people as he seated them. "He continued to be in touch with the entertainers from the Chase almost until his death in July 2003," commented Richard, one of Ulrich's two sons. (Courtesy of Richard Ulrich.)

In 1951, the hotel's main entrance was moved from Lindell to Kingshighway, and the swimming pool was added in the summer of 1954. In 1955, one could spend New Year's Eve at the Chase Club for $5.50 including dinner, dancing, and the floor show.

These entertainers were some of the stars appearing in the Chase Club in the first three months of 1955. (Courtesy of the St. Louis Public Library, Special Collections.)

In 1956, Harold Koplar designed and built the Khorassan Room, named for the mythical potentate, the Veiled Prophet. The elegant room seated 1,000 people and had a 54-foot stage that could be raised and lowered hydraulically. It was the site of the Queen's Supper for many years, beginning in 1957. The October event opened the social season in St. Louis. The Veiled Prophet Ball was held at Kiel Auditorium for 10,000 people, followed by the Queen's Supper in the Khorassan Room. The ball, too, moved to the Chase in 1974, after civil rights demonstrations forced the event from city-owned Kiel Auditorium. This photograph shows the 1964 queen, Miss Alice Busch Condie, presiding at the head table in the Khorassan Room with escorts Kenneth Pierce (left) and Randy Wielandy. (Courtesy of Alice Behan.)

This picture of the Chase newsletter shows the 15th Fleur de Lis Ball with the late John Joseph Cardinal Carberry. The Fleur de Lis Ball, held annually in December in the Khorassan Room, presented debutantes to the archbishop of St. Louis. The formal dinner dance, begun in the late 1950s, raised money to benefit Cardinal Glennon Memorial Hospital for Children. (Courtesy of the St. Louis Public Library, Special Collections.)

Bodies slammed on the canvas floor of the ring in 1959 when Wrestling at the Chase opened in the Khorassan Room. Wrestling was popular during this time with regular matches held at Kiel Auditoriuim. Sam Muchnick, a well-known wrestling promoter, booked the matches at the Chase. Tickets to the show were free, and the audience paid for their buffet dinner and drinks. Crowds filled the elegant room to watch the matches for more than 20 years, and they were broadcast on KPLR-TV. (Courtesy of George Cassimates.)

The Chase was a popular venue for corporate events. Here office girls from Anheuser-Busch, Inc., were can-can dancers during the company's 1959 employee Christmas party in the Khorassan Room. (Courtesy of Mary Ann Spesia, second from the left.)

Marty's Make Believe Ballroom, starring Marty Bronson and Sally King, opened at the Chase in 1974. Buddy and Perri Moreno, who entertained in the Chase Club in the 1950s, sang a few songs on opening night. *Life at the Chase-Park Plaza* reported, "The good old days are back and happy dancers crowd the floor every night as Sal Ferrante plays music of the '40s and '50s."

While dancers glided across the floor on the main level and the Reed Farrell Show, "the Morning Affair," was televised live from the Chase lobby, poodles endured a beauty bath in the lower level. Here Robert Horton (right) brought his two poodles to be groomed by Sam Micotto in the Poodle Palace. (Courtesy of St. Louis Public Library, Special Collections.)

Howls of laughter filled the Khorassan Room when the Advertising Women of St. Louis, Inc., presented its annual gridiron. The show was the brainchild of the late Bea Adams, and yearly performances were played between 1935 and 1987. The shows ended when the Women's Ad Club joined the men's group. The St. Louis shows were the first and largest women's gridiron in the country. St. Louis department store windows displayed some of the costumes. Nothing was sacred to these creative thespians, and the revues of songs, dances, and skits spoofed current events, politicians, and civic leaders. The 1935 show was performed at the Statler. The next year, the group moved to the Coronado and, in later years, the shows were performed at the Chase and the Jefferson Hotels. The proceeds always benefited charitable causes. In 1941, the profits sent 700 blankets to Great Britain for women and children suffering from World War II. In 1942, one thousand women attended the show, and the proceeds bought two ambulances, one for the Red Cross and one for Barnes Hospital. In 1943, the profits turned into war bonds. In later years, money was donated to cancer research. This photograph shows the finale of the March 28, 1973, circus show performed in the Khorassan Room. (Courtesy of Barbara Drant, feathered and perched on the swing.)

The Koplar family sold the Chase and the Park Plaza in 1981. St. Louisan Nick Mucci and his 12-piece band, the Metronomes, played in the Khorassan Room through the years and had a 3-piece strolling group in the lobby in the 1980s. "One night the battery was stolen out of the car of one of my musicians. The neighborhood had started to run down," Mucci recalled. The fashionable Central West End declined, and business at the Chase suffered when new hotels downtown were built. Times had changed and the venerable Chase Hotel had only 25 percent occupancy in 1989. The presidents, the movie stars, the proms, and the debutante balls were ghosts of the past. The Chase closed its doors on September 22, 1989. (Photograph by Gene Donaldson.)

This plate with its copyrighted design was purchased for $1 when the furnishings of the Chase-Park Plaza went on sale to the public. The Park Plaza was converted into apartments, and General Electric Credit Corporation took over the ailing Chase. (Photograph by Gene Donaldson.)

In 1997, James L. Smith, part of Kingsdell, a limited partnership, breathed new life into the Chase when the partnership purchased the hotel from General Electric Credit Corporation and began renovation. Smith is now owner of the Chase. The lobby was restored and, in 1999, a five-screen cinema opened where the Chase Club once was. The Starlight Roof reopened for the new millennium, and one of the early events was a luncheon dance given by a network of Missouri and Illinois hospitals for older adults in the community. This photograph shows Emogene and Vince Beck of Edwardsville, Illinois, at the hospital party. "I always wanted to see what the Starlight Roof looked like," said Mrs. Beck. (Photograph by Joan Roberts of Gateway Regional Medical Center in Granite City, Illinois.)

Steven Becker Fine Dining took over the catering at the Starlight Roof. This photograph shows five waiters and waitresses serving 10 guests at a table simultaneously with a flourish. The hospital-sponsored party in May 2000 was sold out with people anxious to come back to the Chase. (Photograph by Joan Roberts of Gateway Regional Medical Center in Granite City, Illinois.)

This couple was married at the Starlight Roof under the blue neon light shortly after the venue reopened. The blue neon lights that originally backlit the unusual circles and wave-like designs in the ceiling were relit by Steven Becker, caterer. (Photograph by Tom Tussey.)

This photograph, taken from the roof garden extending from the Starlight Roof, shows the Maria Berns wedding reception on May 21, 2005. "For many couples planning the first big party of their married lives, there is no place like a grand hotel," according to the January 1994 issue of *SEEN Magazine*. (Photograph by Nordmann Photography.)

Three

THE MAYFAIR

Now the Roberts Mayfair at Eighth and St. Charles Streets, the Mayfair was listed on the National Register of Historic Places on September 17, 1979. (Courtesy of the Mercantile Library at the University of Missouri–St. Louis.)

According to Pierre Bordes, headwaiter in the Mayfair Room from 1949 to 1955, the Mayfair was born out of a dispute between Charles Heiss, its builder, and Statler. Heiss had managed the Statler in Detroit before transferring to St. Louis to manage the Statler here. When Heiss and Statler differed, Heiss threatened to "build two hotels close to yours and they'll be better than yours," the waiter recalled.

The results of that promise were the Mayfair at St. Charles and Eighth Streets, a block behind the Statler, and the Lennox across Washington Avenue from the Statler. Heiss built both hotels and took William Victor, assistant manager of the Statler, with him when he left.

The Mayfair opened its doors to 120 stockholders and contractors for a reception and dinner on August 29, 1925. The next evening, 4,000 invited guests attended the grand opening and dedication.

St. Louisans applauded Heiss for his splendid accomplishment and local newspapers marked the occasion. *The Censor* reported the opening as an "epoch-making event in the history of St. Louis and predicts for it the success it deserves from an appreciative public."

The paper's prophecy was on target. The Mayfair quickly became a favorite among local residents. The Mayfair Room was among the best restaurants in the country for many years and was the first five-star restaurant in Missouri.

The Mayfair was so proud of its salad dressing that it bore the hotel's name. The Mayfair dressing was first recognized nationally by *Fortune*. It's believed that the anchovy-based dressing was developed about 1935 by chef Fred Bangerter. Gordon Heiss, Charles's son, sold the hotel in the 1970s, but not the dressing recipe. The Mayfair finally retrieved its celebrated dressing 20 years later. Dorothy Smith of St. Louis County recalls craving the Mayfair dressing when she was expecting a baby some 35 years ago. "I made my husband take me to the Mayfair for dinner once a week," she said.

The Prosperity Sandwich was created at the Mayfair by chef and executive steward Eduard Voegeli shortly after the hotel opened, according to Voegeli's grandson. The popular sandwich is still served in the Hofbrau, now known as the Mayfair Bar and Grill. Voegeli also created non-rationed dishes during World War II, and he was featured in the *St. Louis Post-Dispatch* for his sweetbreads en casserole, which he prepared for meatless days.

Laura Elbring, who played the piano in the Mayfair Room in the 1940s, remembered the sweetbreads. "The pay was good and the food was better. The piano was a seven-foot grand painted in antique ivory with cherubs and butterflies," she recalled. A frequent dinner guest at the Mayfair Room took Mrs. Elbring and her husband to Hawaii for 12 days. "He liked that I could play anything he requested," she explained.

The Mayfair was a special place where everyone felt special.

This building at the corner of Eighth and St. Charles Streets was razed to make way for the Mayfair.

This is an early construction photograph of the hotel. Ground was broken on July 5, 1924. The hotel, costing $2.5 million to build, took a little more than a year. A 1925 Model T Ford cost $495. (Courtesy of Carondelet Historical Society.)

Charles Heiss, president of the Mayfair Investment Group, built the hotel and named it for an elite hotel district in London. As a 15-year-old busboy at a hotel in Heidelberg, Germany, Heiss fled the country to escape a famine and dreamed of someday owning his own hotel. He was born in 1883 on a farm outside of Munich and journeyed through hostelries in Belgium, France, England, and Canada before coming to the United States in 1912. The Statler Hotel chain hired Heiss to manage its hotel in Detroit and later transferred him to St. Louis to manage the Statler here. He left after seven years to fulfill the dream of his own hotel. Heiss spoke German, French, and English and knew how to relate to his distinguished clientele. He was in the lobby every day at 7:00 a.m. to greet guests in the old hotel manner. (Courtesy of Barbara Heiss.)

This is the lobby that 4,000 invited guests saw when they attended the grand opening of the Mayfair on August 29, 1925. The hotel, designed by Preston Bradshaw, was built of mat-faced brick with terra cotta trim in the Italian Renaissance style, which was carried into the foyer and lobby with its hand-painted ceiling. All 400 rooms had private baths, and uniformed operators piloted the three high-speed elevators, which were manually operated until the mid-1990s. Crystal chandeliers hung from the copper canopies that covered both the Eighth and St. Charles Street entrances. Three centrifugal pumps with a capacity of one-half million gallons of water a day, enough to serve a town of 15,000 people, provided water for the hotel. When the hotel opened for overnight guests on Sunday, August 30, a traveling man from Chicago was the first to sign the register. He arrived on Thursday, insisting on being the first guest. (Courtesy of Judy Bradshaw Miller.)

This was the mezzanine. Orchestras playing on the mezzanine could be heard throughout the lobby and the dining room. A nine-chair barbershop, six-booth beauty parlor, and chiropodist shop were also on the mezzanine rather than in the basement as in most other hotels. (Courtesy of St. Louis Public Library, Fine Arts Department.)

This luxurious lounge on the mezzanine was an outstanding feature of the Mayfair. Its homelike atmosphere invited guests to rest or receive company outside their rooms. Red silk draperies covered the windows. Two private dining rooms and a ladies' retiring room were also on this floor. (Courtesy of Judy Bradshaw Miller.)

The Heiss family lived at the Mayfair. These are the two Heiss children, Jean and C. Gordon. "We lived at the Mayfair until I was 12 years old," said Jean Heiss Donegan. "We had three connecting bedrooms, a little kitchen, and a living room. My mother tried to keep us busy, but we still managed to throw food out the window," she smiled. "I was the Eloise of the Mayfair," she said referring to the fictional, six-year-old resident of the Plaza Hotel in New York City. Her brother, Gordon, assumed ownership of the hotel from his father in the mid-1950s and successfully managed it for 25 years. He was well known to many St. Louisans. Massachusetts Mutual Life Insurance Company took the hotel over in the 1970s and placed it on the market for $950,000, $1.5 million less than it cost to build. Gordon Heiss died in 1995 at age 70 in Santa Fe, New Mexico. This photograph was taken on the corner of Eighth and St. Charles Streets next to the hotel. The Mayfair is not in view. (Courtesy of Jean Donegan.)

This advertisement emphasized value for your money. Room rates ranged from $3 to $6 a night when the hotel opened, and each room had all the finery of the day, including an outside exposure, bath, circulating ice water, an electric fan, a bed lamp, and a large closet. Three shops with entrances on Eighth Street included a telegraph office. The cigar store and haberdashery connected with the lobby for guests' convenience. (Courtesy of Carondelet Historical Society.)

The attractive coffee shop, located in the basement and finished in decorative tile, later became the hotel's laundry. (Courtesy of St. Louis Public Library, Fine Arts Department.)

Dinner in the Mayfair Room was a memorable experience. It had sparkling crystal, two white linen tablecloths on each table, and Elizabethan décor. The enormous silver serving pieces were called "the family jewels" by the hotel manager. Steak Diane, a specialty of the Mayfair, was included in a 1965 book, *Famous Foods From Famous Places*. Named for the goddess of the hunt, the prime sirloin cut was seared and sautéed in butter with shallots and mushrooms toasting alongside. Then the whole entrée was flamed with brandy. According to Marian O'Brien, *St. Louis Globe-Democrat* food editor at the time, "There sometimes is so much brandy aflame in the Mayfair Room that one can't help but hope that it won't get out of hand!" (Courtesy of Judy Bradshaw Miller.)

Mayfair chef Eduard Voegeli gives Atlantic City beauty pageant contestants a cooking lesson in this photo. The chef spoke seven languages. He was born in Switzerland, apprenticed as a pastry chef in France, then moved to England to join the Royal Navy. He worked in hotels in Canada, New York, and Pennsylvania before coming to St. Louis. Voegeli was founder and first president of the Chefs de Cuisine Association.

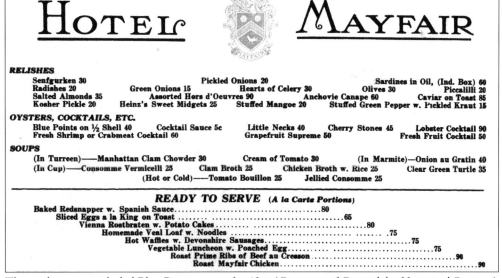

HOTEL MAYFAIR

RELISHES

Senfgurken 30	Pickled Onions 20	Sardines in Oil, (Ind. Box) 60
Radishes 20	Green Onions 15	Hearts of Celery 30	Olives 30	Piccalilli 20
Salted Almonds 35	Assorted Hors d'Oeuvres 90	Anchovie Canape 60	Caviar on Toast 85
Kosher Pickle 20	Heinz's Sweet Midgets 25	Stuffed Mangoe 20	Stuffed Green Pepper w. Pickled Kraut 15

OYSTERS, COCKTAILS, ETC.

Blue Points on ½ Shell 40	Cocktail Sauce 5c	Little Necks 40	Cherry Stones 45	Lobster Cocktail 90
Fresh Shrimp or Crabmeat Cocktail 60		Grapefruit Supreme 50		Fresh Fruit Cocktail 50

SOUPS

(In Turreen)——Manhattan Clam Chowder 30	Cream of Tomato 30	(In Marmite)——Onion au Gratin 40
(In Cup)——Consomme Vermicelli 25	Clam Broth 25	Chicken Broth w. Rice 25	Clear Green Turtle 35
(Hot or Cold)——Tomato Bouillon 25	Jellied Consomme 25	

READY TO SERVE (A la Carte Portions)

Baked Redsnapper w. Spanish Sauce	.80
Sliced Eggs a la King on Toast	.65
Vienna Rostbraten w. Potato Cakes	.80
Homemade Veal Loaf w. Noodles	.75
Hot Waffles w. Devonshire Sausages	.75
Vegetable Luncheon w. Poached Egg	.75
Roast Prime Ribs of Beef au Cresson	.90
Roast Mayfair Chicken	.90

This early menu included Blue Point oysters for 40¢. (Courtesy of Carondelet Historical Society.)

Corner of the Hofbrau -- Hotel Mayfair -- Saint Louis

3A-H1064

The Hofbrau opened in 1934 with the repeal of Prohibition. The Hofbrau frequently won *Holiday Magazine* awards for distinguished dining in the 1960s. Count Henry Hoffmann presided over the long bar. His designation as the "Count" symbolized the nobility of the drinks he mixed. He was known as guide, philosopher, and friend to bar patrons. This genial host was a master of the cocktail shaker and, though he never drank, he trained many younger men in his art. In pre-Prohibition days, he was known as the "Michelangelo of St. Louis Bartenders." Count Hoffmann was also rated as St. Louis's number one baseball fan. For many years, he placed his order with Cardinals management on opening day of the season for $1,000 worth of World Series tickets. He organized parties that traveled on special trains to other cities to attend World Series games. The famous bartender, age 66, died of an apparent heart attack in a box at Sportsman's Park in the 17th inning of a tie game between the Cardinals and the Giants on April 30, 1936. (Courtesy of St. Louis Public Library, Special Collections.)

These beverages, including near beers, were served in the Mayfair dining room during Prohibition. The 18th Amendment (Prohibition) to the Constitution was passed in 1918. For those who were counting, it was 13 years, 10 months, 19 days, and 17 hours before the Prohibition Amendment was repealed.

Beverage List

Gingerales

	Pt.
Anheuser-Busch	.30
Anheuser-Busch Pale Dry	.45
Canada Dry	.45
Clicquot Club Dry	.45
Falstaff Pale Dry	.30
White Rock Pale Dry	.45

Still and Sparkling Waters

	Qt.	Pt.
Appollinaries	70	40
Lemon Soda		30
Poland Water	50	
Welsh's Grape Juice	1.50	1.00
White Rock Water	65	35
Coca Cola		.15
Grape Juice, Ind. Bottle		.30
Grape Bouquet		.25
Mountain Mist		.50
Root Beer		.25

Near Beers

Budweiser	.25
Falstaff Super X	.25
Malt Nutrine	.30
Pilsener or Muenchener	.25

Egg and Milk Drinks

Chocolate Egg Malted Milk	.40
Chocolate Malted Milk	.25
Egg Chocolate Milk	.35
Egg Malted Milk	.35
Egg Flipp	.30
Plain Malted Milk	.25

Lemonade and Fruit Drinks
Made from Fresh Fruit

Cherry Lemonade	.30
Fruit Lemonade	.30
Grape Juice Punch	.35
Lemonade	.25
Limeade	.35
Lemon or Lime each	.10
Orangeade	.30
Sweet Cider, Glass	.15

	1-2 Pt.	Pt.
Pure Orange Juice	60	1.20
Pure Lemon Juice	60	1.20

Cocktails

Apricot or White Grape Juice	.30
Vermouth or Grenadine	.30

Served in Dining Room and Guests Rooms

Count Hoffmann and his bartenders stood ready to serve in 1934 when Prohibition ended. (Courtesy of Carondelet Historical Society.)

This is a close-up view of one of the stained glass windows in the Hofbrau bar. The vibrant windows illustrated lute players, imbibing gentlemen, and bashful maidens. The Hofbrau was decorated with German murals, a reminder of the hotel's European influence. (Photograph by Gene Donaldson.)

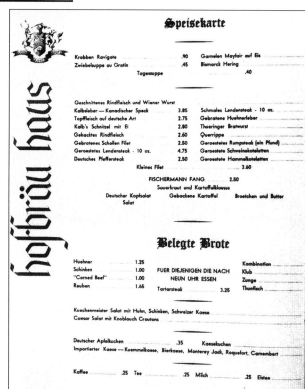

In the early days, the Hofbrau menu was printed in German and in English. (Courtesy of the Carondelet Historical Society.)

It is our policy
not to serve
UNESCORTED
LADIES

These items were printed by the hotel in its early days. (Courtesy of the Carondelet Historical Society.)

The Exacting Requirements of Hotel Mayfair for
CAB SERVICE
Stressing-Reliability-Honesty-Courtesy were easily met by the

RED TOP CAB CO.
FOREST
4500

YELLOW CAB CO.
FOREST
1234

CHECKER CAB CO.
LINDELL
123

American Legion

Convention

SEPTEMBER 23-26, 1935

Hotel Mayfair

SAINT LOUIS

This was the cover of convention material.

This was the hotel's stationery in its early days. (Courtesy of the Carondelet Historical Society.)

Hotel Mayfair

KMOX Radio went on the air in 1925 in this studio on the mezzanine of the Mayfair. The inset photos are Jacquinot Jules (left), musical director of KMOX, organist, and accompanist; Miss Alice Maslin, program director who also played dinnertime recitals; and George Junkin, director and announcer. KMOX installed an $18,000 Kilgen organ, and recitals were played from the organ loft every day at noon and between 6:00 and 7:00 p.m., according to Frank Absher, station historian. In 1931, KMOX left the Mayfair for larger quarters and opened studios in the Mart Building. (Courtesy of St. Louis Public Library, Media Archives.)

THE VOICE OF ST. LOUIS

JACQUINOT JULES, Musical Director

ALICE MASLIN, Program Director

KMOX MAIN STUDIO

Jean Heiss, daughter of the Mayfair's owner, was about four years old when she wished everyone a merry Christmas from the hotel over KMOX Radio. The microphone is on a curved stand in front of Jean. The gentlemen are unidentified KMOX employees. (Courtesy of Jean Heiss Donegan.)

Torchy, a pianist who played in a syncopated style, took the Mayfair, KMOX, and St. Louis by storm. "Torchy at the piano in the KMOX studio became so popular that she replaced the organ recitals," said Frank Absher. Honorine LaPee was born in 1904 in Sullivan, Missouri, where she began piano lessons. She started her career accompanying the silent movies shown at her brother's theatre. She came to St. Louis and spent a year at Visitation Academy studying music. She signed a contract with KMOX, and the vivacious pianist soon became the station's leading listener attraction. One of her fans thought the auburn-haired beauty should be nicknamed "Torchy," and it stuck.

Torchy was one of 11 children, and she and three of her sisters formed a band called the Music Makers. Cecelia on violin (left), Torchy on piano, Frances on saxophone, and Mary Katherine on drums played at local establishments. Torchy also played with the Gordon Jenkins band.

This window display pronounced Torchy winner of the national KMOX popularity contest sponsored by Whiting Tours in 1926. Her prize was a trip to Havana, Cuba. KMOX received piles of requests every day, and her time on the air was increased so she could answer the requests. The station prepared photographs that she autographed and sent to her fans across the country. She played at the Coliseum and various theatres in St. Louis.

At the end of her KMOX contract, Torchy left St. Louis and resumed playing with her own band. She married, raised three daughters, and moved to Washington, Missouri, where she played on KWRE Radio. In her 70s, she played four-hour gigs at the Town and Country Bowling Alley in Washington. In her early 80s, she visited one of her daughters and had dinner in a restaurant that had a piano. She immediately sat down to play and the owner offered her a job, according to her daughter. Torchy died at age 83 in 1987. (Courtesy of Gail Kingsbury, Torchy's daughter.)

Julia Runge King, "first lady" and manager of the Mayfair, worked for the hotel for 50 years. The hotel had been open three years when she started her career there at 16 in the accounting department. Julia King rose through the ranks and was named to the top spot in 1957, the first woman manager of a hotel in St. Louis. In true Mayfair tradition, she was in the lobby at mealtimes meeting and greeting guests. Her friendly and outgoing manner endeared her guests to the hotel. She later became vice president of Mayfair-Lennox Hotels, Inc., and managed the Lennox along with the Mayfair.

Cary Grant wired holiday greetings to Julia King in 1963. "She used to let him come into the hotel through a back door and use the freight elevator to get to his floor," remembered the late Monsignor Fenton Runge, King's brother. Cary Grant's legacy to the Mayfair is said to be the chocolate on your pillow, a tradition he started in the 1950s. The Mayfair continued the tradition, and it spread to hotels across the country. Julia King's uncanny ability to remember names and faces amazed many a guest. The *St. Louis Globe-Democrat*, in a 1933 feature story on her, reported the arrival of a guest from Seattle. The tall, stately young woman greeted him by name and said, "You may have your old room—1305." She had not seen the gentleman since he stayed at the hotel three years earlier. During her career, she often said, "There's no business like show business . . . except maybe the hotel business." (Courtesy of the Carondelet Historical Society.)

In the summer of 1961, the Mayfair opened the first rooftop swimming pool in St. Louis, 250 feet above the city sidewalk. Orange trees, geraniums, ageratum, and a fountain brightened the pool area. Fashion-model lifeguards with bouffant hairdos and black lace swimsuits were attractions. In 1991, the pool won the National Pool and Spa Association's Renovation Award. The same year the pool opened, an all-girl barbershop debuted in the hotel. But former attorney general Thomas Eagleton closed it down, declaring the "barberettes" were cosmetologists, not barbers. (Courtesy of the Carondelet Historical Society.)

In 1960, the Bar Association of St. Louis opened one of the plushest headquarters of any local group on the 18th floor of the Mayfair. Since law as practiced in America derived from English common law, the quarters had an English accent. This photograph shows the main dining room that was paneled in Georgian pine and lighted by three English crystal chandeliers. Paneling throughout the club was originally used in English manor houses and castles, and cut to blueprint dimensions in Great Britain. In another dining room, the waiters' weskits of wool plaid, specially woven in Scotland, matched the draperies. Old parchment documents and engravings of prominent English barristers decorated the walls of the headquarters. (Courtesy of the Bar Association of Metropolitan St. Louis.)

Sorkis Webbe Jr. (left) and his father bought the Mayfair in 1977 and St. Louisans could breathe a sigh of relief. The younger Webbe had shined shoes in the Mayfair lobby as a boy. The Mayfair was still prominent in the 1960s. A lavish ball for Rose Kennedy was held in the Mayfair Room while 25¢ happy hour drinks were served in the Hofbrau. In 1968, the Mayfair was home to the national Governors' Conference. But in the 1970s, downtown patrons were few. Legitimate theater was passé at the American Theater and movies at the Loews State and Ambassador Theaters played to slim crowds. Travelers, too, opted to stay at hotels farther west. The hotel passed through a series of owners and the bar association left in 1977, when the rate for a single room was $18 a night. The Webbes, leaders in the local Democratic Party, spent $3.5 million renovating the hotel. They gutted the rooms, tore out inner walls, and enlarged them. The number of rooms dropped from the original 400 to 230. They restored the hand-painted ceiling in the lobby. In later years, the hand painting was covered with plaster. The Mayfair's six-door Cadillac limousine picked guests up at the airport. "We have set out to create a difference between just checking into a hotel and staying at the Mayfair," Webbe Jr. said at the time. When the hotel opened its doors for Architects' Sunday in February 1979, more than 700 people lined up along St. Charles Street, to tour St. Louis's showplace. (Courtesy of Patricia Webbe.)

This advertisement, which appeared in the *St. Louis Post-Dispatch*, shows Emmitt, the uniformed doorman, and an unidentified model. The Webbes opened the Gaslight Club in the venerable Mayfair Room. It was a branch of the Chicago-based club, the nation's original key club, and the first in St. Louis. The owners retained the integrity of the room itself, although glamorous, scantily-clad "Gaslight girls" served drinks, and belly dancers swayed during lunchtime. (Courtesy of Patricia Webbe.)

Part of the Webbe renovation included these chandeliers, moved from the Aladdin in Las Vegas, which they also owned, and hung in the lobby of the Mayfair. The chandeliers still glitter and are the focus of attention upon entering the hotel. By 1983, the Webbes owned the Gateway (formerly the Statler) and the Lennox and had visions of redeveloping Washington Avenue. But Webbe Jr.'s political activities interrupted his plans. FBI wiretaps in his office at the hotel led to federal indictments, and the Webbes lost the hotel. They left their mark, however, turning the direction of the hotel and setting the stage for its future. (Photograph by Gene Donaldson.)

The Roberts brothers bought the Mayfair for about $4.5 million in 2003 from Wyndham International Inc., which had acquired it through a merger in 1998. They removed part of the marble floor in the lobby and inserted their name. The Roberts brothers purchased the American Theater from the original owner's family and renamed it the Roberts Orpheum Theater. It opened in 1917 and was called the Orpheum. The brothers currently own television and broadcast companies and a number of other properties that they are redeveloping. (Photograph by Gene Donaldson.)

The Roberts installed this Egyptian work of art in a sculpture niche on the hotel mezzanine. "Our top priority is gaining a five-star ranking . . . and returning the facility to its original glamour and opulence," Steven Roberts told a *St. Louis Post-Dispatch* reporter at the time of purchase. (Photograph by Gene Donaldson.)

Four

THE CORONADO

Now Coronado Place, at Lindell and Spring Avenues, the Coronado was listed on the National Register of Historic Places for Midtown District on July 7, 1978. (Courtesy of Judy Bradshaw Miller.)

It was 1939 when two unusual guests registered at the luxurious, million-dollar Coronado Hotel—a bear cub and its owner. The gentleman attended a shoe convention, and the animal represented the company's sales slogan: "Bear Down For Fall." Unfortunately the cub escaped from his cage, sending lobby guests and clerks scurrying in all directions. The bear's keeper finally caught it after a whirlwind chase through the revolving doors at the front entrance.

The hotel was built in stages from 1923 to 1929 and officially opened in 1925. It was quickly embraced by the public, then Charleston-dancing flappers and their slick-haired escorts. Important figures like Franklin D. Roosevelt, Charles Lindbergh (after his solo flight to Paris), and Harry S. Truman chose the Coronado for their St. Louis stays. Celebrities like silent-movie stars Lew Cody and Mabel Norman, opera singer Mary Garden, actress Ilka Chase, and cowboy star Tom Mix also bedded down at the Coronado.

Through the years, St. Louisans gravitated to the hotel to celebrate special occasions. Bob and Irene Enkelmann of St. Louis had dinner at the Coronado when Bob received a $10 a month raise from Union Electric after passing his new-employee, six-month probation period in 1956.

Bix Beiderbecke, legendary jazz trumpeter of the 1920s, came to the Coronado to listen to the bands during his off hours at the Arcadia Ballroom, later called Tune Town. When a customer threw peanut shells into a tuba, Blue Steele, the band leader and ex-prizefighter, walked off the bandstand and punched the offender in the nose.

Nick Mucci and his band played at the hotel. Mucci remembers the Jug, an elegant restaurant and cocktail lounge. "They had violinists in three corners of the room and an accordionist in the fourth corner," he recalled.

But the good life was not destined to last forever and in a moment of ignominy, the venerable Coronado Hotel was sold at a foreclosure auction on the steps of the Civil Courts Building in 1964. Workmen turned off the electricity and telephone service. The water bill was long overdue. About 100 tenants hauled their belongings to the street while porters picketed for back wages. The city building commissioner attached a condemned sign to the building and padlocked the door in the interest of safety.

St. Louis University bought the hotel in 1964 and converted it into a school dormitory. The main dining room became the cafeteria and the Jug was an indoor recreation room. The university sold it to Sterling Properties in 1986 and the once-grand Coronado would sit vacant for the next 15 years.

A young couple, Amrit and Amy Gill of Restoration St. Louis, Inc., purchased the complex in 2001. By that time, a wall had collapsed, part of the roof was gone and rubble was chest deep, according to Landmarks Association. The Gills spent $40 million to restore it, and reopened it in December 2003. The ballroom and series of lobbies have been meticulously restored and are open for inspection. In addition, the Coronado has restaurants, office space, and 165 apartments.

The cover photograph on this book shows the original entrance to the hotel. Through exacting restoration, the lobby now looks the same, except the fountain in the center has been replaced by a table and a floral arrangement.

The circle driveway led to the canopied entrance that faced Lindell Boulevard. The hotel rose 14 stories and had 600 rooms.

A long and decorative lobby stretched across the front of the building. A fireplace is still there on the west wall of the lobby. The hotel printed a booklet with a dark green velvet cover when the hotel opened. It read, "Like all supremely successful architectural creations, this hotel belongs in a distinctive rank of its own in hotel construction. This great structure of modern free style design is situated on the crest of the city on the fashionable thoroughfare, Lindell Boulevard. One studies with ever-increasing pleasure its harmony and beauty." (Courtesy of Judy Bradshaw Miller.)

This elaborate lounge invited guests to rest and savor its elegance. The floor lamps are complete with fringed shades, typical of the 1920s.

The Application of all Plain and Ornamental Plastering and the Erection of all Lathing and Partition Work were included in our Contract for the Coronado Hotel.

LOUNGE ❖ CORONADO HOTEL

Other contracts completed for Mr. Bradshaw by us, are:
Melbourne Hotel
Dorr & Zeller Building
Forest Park Hotel
of St. Louis
and Bellerive Hotel
of Kansas City

P. Rowan & Sons Plastering Co.

The plastering company was so proud of its work that it used the Coronado in future advertisements. (Courtesy of Judy Bradshaw Miller.)

The ballroom with its ornate vaulted ceiling and square lights shining through the marble floor was the scene of many parties. The hotel's booklet read, "The Hotel Coronado has become an authentic setting for the social activities and day-by-day life of most exclusive St. Louisans and their visiting guests. A house physician is constantly in attendance for our guests."

Sparkling crystal chandeliers lighted the main dining room. (Courtesy of Judy Bradshaw Miller.)

The Grille Room was on the eastern edge of the hotel with exposures to Spring Avenue and Lindell Boulevard. It has been restored to its original look and a Spring Avenue entrance leads to the Nadoz Café.

The side entrance (Spring Avenue) opened to the Grille Room, which was the hotel's coffee shop. (Courtesy of Judy Bradshaw Miller.)

An orchestra played for dinner on the patio. (Courtesy of the St. Louis Public Library, Special Collections.)

The patio faced Lindell just west of the hotel entrance. It is now Joe Boccardi's Ristorante with indoor and outdoor seating. (Courtesy of Judy Bradshaw Miller.)

The Supper Club

The Pal-Lido, Coronado's Supper Club, is one of the outstanding rooms of the country, known from coast to coast for excellent cuisine and delightful music. It is the gathering place for those who enjoy dancing and entertainment in an atmosphere of refinement.

Ever-changing entertainment, together with nationally-known orchestras, tends to keep a high degree of interest during the winter season.

There is full orchestration for luncheon, dinner and supper with a Sunday evening concert from 6:00 to 9:00 p. m.

This page was part of the hotel booklet. It also stated, "Music may be transmitted to any of the private party rooms, at will, by amplifiers from the Pal-Lido and the central radio receiving apparatus." In the 1930s, big bands played at the Coronado, including Duke Ellington and Isham Jones. When Jones needed a fill-in pianist, he hired a Webster Groves man named Gordon Jenkins. Jones liked Jenkins's playing so well that he took him along on his tour, and Jenkins got his start nationally. (Courtesy of St. Louis Public Library, Special Collections.)

Thanksgiving 1930

Thursday, November 27th

Pal-Lido

Grand hotels were popular places for families celebrating holidays. (Courtesy of St. Louis Public Library, Special Collections.)

THANKSGIVING DINNER $2.50
Served From 12 To 9 P.M.

FRUIT SUPREME

CAPE COD OYSTER COCKTAIL   CANAPE PRISCILLA

GIBLET SOUP OLD FASHIONED   CREAM OF TOMATO PROFITROLE
CONSOMME PURITAN

CELERY   GREEN OLIVES   RADISHES

HALF LOBSTER STANDISH
ROAST GOOSE, SPICED PEACH
BAKED VIRGINIA HAM, CIDER SAUCE
ROAST SUCKLING PIG, APPLE AND RAISIN DRESSING
ROAST VT. TURKEY, CHESTNUT DRESSING, CRANBERRY SAUCE

CANDIED SWEET POTATOES   NEW GARDEN PEAS

SALAD MAYFLOWER

MINCE PIE   PLUM PUDDING, BRANDY SAUCE   PUMPKIN PIE
GLACE NESSELRODE

RAISINS   DATES   FIGS   NUTS

APPLE CIDER

COFFEE

The hotel's advertisement in the 1920s set the Coronado apart from other hotels. Its proximity to the new Grand Avenue theater district enhanced its popularity. The bottom of the ad reads, "The apex of extravagance in comfort, the acme of economy in charge." (Courtesy of St. Louis Public Library, Special Collections.)

Preston J. Bradshaw designed, owned, and managed the Coronado. He was a nationally known architect from the Midwest for nearly four decades. Bradshaw was born in St. Louis in 1884. His father was a grain broker. He graduated from Columbia College and Barnard College for Architecture in New York City. He returned to St. Louis at age 23 and began his illustrious career. He designed the Mayfair, the Lennox, the Chase, the Melbourne, the Senate, and the Congress hotels in St. Louis as well as many apartment buildings and homes in the Central West End. He also drew plans for the Brown Hotel in Louisville, Kentucky, and the Baker Hotel in Dallas, Texas. His local credits include the Paul Brown Building, the Mart Building, Glen Echo Country Club, and the St. Louis County Courthouse in Clayton. He also left his mark on Washington, D.C., when he designed the House and Senate buildings. Bradshaw married Hilda Werner and the couple had two daughters. The family lived at the Coronado and at a farm in Gray Summit, Missouri. He died at age 72 of an apparent heart attack in his room at the Coronado in 1953 with his wife and one of his daughters in an adjoining room. He is buried in Calvary Cemetery. The beauty of the restored Coronado is testimony to his talent. (Courtesy of Judy Bradshaw Miller.)

Visitors to the Coronado were greeted by this ornate lobby. When Queen Marie of Romania stayed at there in 1926, the hotel converted the entire 14th floor as her suite. They embroidered the royal crest of Romania on the linens and had a special mattress made for her with three times the usual amount of feathers. Unfortunately, the mattress was lumpy and the queen fell out of bed three times during the night, according to an article that appeared in the *St. Louis Globe-Democrat* in 1968. At 1:00 a.m., she finally retired to her private train car in Union Station to complete her night's rest.

On November 19, 1937, another distinguished guest checked in at the Coronado—Eleanor Roosevelt. The Bradshaw family has kept the original registration sheet. (Courtesy of Judy Bradshaw Miller.)

A year later, Margaret Korte and her husband-to-be had dinner at the Coronado, and she took a tablecloth home as a souvenir. "Nobody had any money in those days and it was a big deal to go to the Coronado," explained Margaret Korte Unger. In 1944, she enlisted in the Women's Marine Corps, worked at Marine Court Headquarters in Washington, D.C., and rose to staff sergeant. (Courtesy of Margaret Unger.)

Margaret Unger still has the frayed and worn tablecloth from almost 70 years ago. The insignia "the Jug" is still plainly stamped on the fabric. The Jug was a popular restaurant and cocktail lounge in the lower level of the hotel. In the summer, guests spilled out onto the patio. (Photograph by Gene Donaldson.)

Francisco Vasquez de Coronado is also pictured on the tablecloth. Bradshaw named his hotel after the 16th century Spanish explorer, the second hotel to bear his name. The first was the Hotel del Coronado built in 1888 in San Diego, California. (Photograph by Gene Donaldson.)

In 1947, the Sheraton Corporation of America acquired controlling interest in the hotel. It was valued at $2.5 million at that time, and Bradshaw stepped down from resident director to vice president of the Sheraton Corporation. (Courtesy of St. Louis Public Library, Special Collections.)

Life went on as usual at the Coronado. This picture shows the St. Louis Dental Assistants Society installing new officers in 1962 in a candlelight ceremony. (Courtesy of Diane May, fourth from right, who was elected treasurer.)

The Rebirth of a Saint Louis Treasure

YOU ARE CORDIALLY INVITED TO ATTEND

THE GRAND REOPENING OF THE

Coronado Ballroom

DECEMBER 3, 2003

6:30–10:30 PM

3701 LINDELL BOULEVARD

SAINT LOUIS, MISSOURI

~

HOSTED BY:

AMRIT AND AMY GILL

STEVE AND KATHY BECKER

~

MUSIC BY THE FABULOUS MOTOWN REVUE

~

KINDLY RESPOND BY NOVEMBER 24

(314) 367-4848 EXT: 109

The invitation for the reopening of the Coronado ballroom was tucked in a gold folder and tied with a ribbon. When the Gills purchased the derelict building in 2001 and announced plans to renovate it, people with fond memories of the hotel were elated and skeptics wondered if it would ever be accomplished. The grand reopening dispelled any doubts. About 900 guests filled the 10,000-square-foot ballroom, including a balcony level, and marveled at the restoration. The original terrazzo floor was uncovered and restored and the 45 square up-lights on the floor were repaired and shined brightly. Judy Miller, Preston Bradshaw's daughter, presented the Gills with a portrait of her father in gratitude for their work. Of all the buildings Bradshaw designed, this one had a special place in his heart, Miller said, according to the *West End Word* that covered the grand reopening. The portrait now hangs in the hotel. Ron Elz (Johnny Rabbitt), radio personality, remembered broadcasting from a studio in the Coronado in the 1950s and early 1960s. (Courtesy of Judy Miller.)

Bill and Elaine Wolff were married in the Coronado ballroom on March 9, 1948, with the reception following the ceremony. "The Coronado was the 'in' spot in those days," Mrs. Wolff said. "It was beautiful. The ballroom was decorated with gardenia trees," she remembered. The hotel pastry chef prepared a four-and-a-half-foot cake, a replica of Queen Elizabeth II's wedding

cake. Swan ice sculptures highlighted the room and Bonnie Ross and his band played for the several hundred guests. The bride and groom are seated in the center of the head table across from the cake. (Courtesy of Bill and Elaine Wolff.)

The Wolffs returned to the Coronado in December 2003, invited by the Gills for the reopening. The couple, who lives in west St. Louis County, affectionately remembered the hotel's restaurants, the Coal Hole and the Jug. The restoration seems faithful, and the only obvious difference is that the new ballroom is better lit, Mrs. Wolff said at the reopening party. (Courtesy of the West End Word; photograph by Marian Brickner.)

This view of the ballroom as it looks today is from the foyer. (Photograph by Gene Donaldson.)

These ladies have lunch on the patio where generations of guests preceded them. (Photograph by Gene Donaldson.)

A young man sitting on a sofa in the foreground pecks on a laptop computer in the restored Coronado lounge. The arched opening at the far end leads to the lobby. Landmarks Association of St. Louis, Inc., honored the restoration of the Coronado Hotel as one of 11 special projects receiving awards. The award ceremony was held May 10, 2004, at the Coronado. (Photograph by Gene Donaldson.)

Five

THE LENNOX

Now the Renaissance St. Louis Suites Hotel at Washington Avenue and Ninth Street, it was listed on the National Register of Historic Places on September 6, 1984. (Courtesy of St. Louis Mercantile Library at the University of Missouri–St. Louis.)

Charles Heiss kept his promise to build two hotels to compete with the Statler when ground was broken for the Lennox in 1928. Calvin Coolidge was the 30th president of the United States. Prohibition was already 10 years old, and bare knuckles rapped on speakeasy doors. Bessie Smith sang the blues, and Jelly Roll Morton introduced jazz to enthusiastic audiences.

On the heels of his success at the Mayfair, Heiss's new hotel was to be operated as a commercial hotel with 32 sample rooms occupying most of one floor. The Lennox had no ballroom or large banquet hall, but no expense was spared for beauty. It took 18 months and a then-staggering $2.5 million to build the 25-story, 400-room hotel designed by Preston Bradshaw. At that time, it was the tallest hotel in St. Louis. The Lennox marked the end of the hotel construction boom.

When Heiss left the Statler, he took with him William Victor, assistant manager, who took over the operation of the Lennox.

The hotel opened just weeks before the stock market crash. At the grand opening September 2–3, 1929, Charles Heiss treated thousands of invited guests to receptions and buffet suppers. Eager guests were admitted by card. A newspaper account of the opening commented that nothing was spared to make the hotel a fine example of the decorator's art.

In addition to the public dining room, there were three private dining rooms. The coffee shop in the basement was of period Spanish with buff walls and a ceiling studded with heavy oak beams. The coffee shop, the main dining room, and the barber shop were artificially cooled. The mechanical air-cooling system regulated the air inside the hotel according to the air outside and marked the hotel as the last word in construction.

Hand telephone sets were used throughout the hotel. The Lennox was the only hotel west of Chicago operated entirely by electricity, including an electric refrigeration plant.

Musicians from the St. Louis Symphony played at the grand opening, and it was broadcast on KMOX Radio, then only four years old. The stage was set for another stunning success for Charles Heiss.

The Lennox was home to Clara Bow, the "It Girl" of the movie screen, when she and her husband visited St. Louis in 1937. The hotel was also home to the Gordon Heiss family. Gordon took over management of the hotel from his father, Charles. St. Louisan Barbara Heiss, Gordon's daughter, said, "I was brought home from the hospital to the third floor of the Lennox and lived there until I was three years old. We had a four-horse merry-go-round in the playroom on the third floor. We walked the dog down the fire escape and had room service for dinner. I learned how to push the elevator button and sometimes went down to the lobby in a diaper, looking for candy."

In a twist of fate, the Lennox, built to compete with its hotel neighbor across the street, joined its formal rival under the Renaissance Hotel Corporation banner.

The Lennox made history even during construction. A new method of digging foundation wells for skyscrapers was used in the excavation for the hotel, the first time this method was used in St. Louis. A boring machine dug through 45 feet of clay and quicksand to solid rock in less than eight hours. Thirty-six 45-foot wells were dug for the piers and filled with water to prevent cave-ins. A diver prepared the bottom of each well for a one-foot-thick concrete base, which was poured through a pipe and allowed to set under water. A corrugated lining was inserted in the hole, the water was pumped out, and the building of the piers, which supported the 25 stories, was completed. The Lennox was built with a basement and a sub-basement. (Courtesy of the Missouri Historical Society, St. Louis; photograph by Block Brothers, 1929.)

Guests stepped into the lobby of solid mahogany paneling that reached to the high ceiling molded in bright colors. Heavy green brocade drapes enhanced the English effect of the lobby and mezzanine. (Courtesy of Historic Restoration Properties, Inc.)

This early advertisement touted circulating ice water, electric fans, and a free morning paper under your door. The guest rooms were furnished in period English with bathtub and shower, easy chairs, and floor and reading lamps. Room rates started at $2.50 a night when the hotel opened. In 1935, the Lennox advertised its weekend trip. The package included a ticket to either an American or National League baseball game, a ticket to the Municipal Opera, an excursion on a Mississippi River steamboat, six meals and lodging—all for $12.50. In 1937, guest-controlled air conditioning and RCA radios were added to the rooms. Visitors could listen to Fibber McGee and Molly in the comfort of their cool rooms. (Courtesy of the Carondelet Historical Society.)

"These rooms are more than over-sized telephone booths!"

"Yes, and they haven't that stereotyped appearance either!

Refinement and comfort at low cost

Full Length Mirrors, Beauty Rest Mattresses, Bed and Bridge Lamps, Smokers' Stands, Tie, Trouser and Shoe Racks, Circulating Ice-Water, Electric Fans, Hand Set Telephones, Chain Door Locks, and a Free Morning Paper under the door each day.

The tasteful appointments, modern refinements, and thoughtful innovations found in all Lennox rooms and suites, are those usually found only in higher priced rooms. A partial list of them appears at the left.

HOTEL LENNOX

"In the center of things"

The Bodega was the coffee shop in the basement and one of two Lennox restaurants in the early 1930s. One of their ads read, "Step in out of the Depression," said the corkscrew with a grin, "Fuller living finds expression in the restaurants within!"

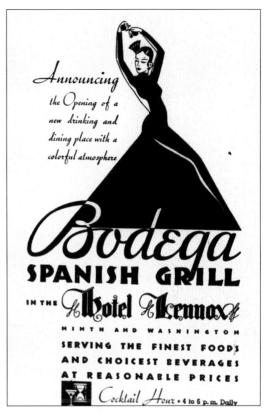

One of their specialties was lamp chop imperial. (Courtesy of the Carondelet Historical Society.)

In the late 1930s, the Spanish Bodega in the basement was redecorated and named the Rathskeller. A 30-foot bar was installed along the east wall, and built-in seats lined the west wall. People with advance reservations for opening night overflowed the room. Baritone Wayne Fletcher and pianist Herme Zinzer entertained diners in St. Louis's newest drinking and dining establishment. At its peak, six bartenders zigzagged behind the long bar mixing drinks for a packed house. Nightly entertainment changed every two weeks. An early luncheon menu listed tongue cutlets with creamed spinach and parsley potato for 45¢. Some people remember the Rathskeller for its resin-baked potatoes. (Courtesy of Historic Restoration, Inc. Properties.)

Three murals in the Rathskeller depicted exploration of the Western world. This one shows DeSoto at the Mississippi River. The other two illustrated Balboa at the Pacific Ocean and Christopher Columbus discovering America.

Eduard Voegeli, executive chef at the Lennox and Mayfair, demonstrated carving at Stix, Baer, and Fuller Department Store in November 1945 before Thanksgiving. The catchy copy included, "If your roasts deserve the Purple Heart, this is your meat." (Courtesy of the Carondelet Historical Society.)

Charles Heiss owned both the Mayfair and the Lennox, and this combined Christmas card was mailed during World War II. The Lennox made headlines in 1944 when the employees bought $8,175 worth of war bonds and set up a booth in the lobby to sell war bonds to guests. The hotel received a citation from the U. S. Treasury Department for its efforts. That same year, a wartime boom for rooms filled the hotels. The Lennox, which catered to conventions, used its display rooms to accommodate guests. Five or six soldiers slept in a room normally used for sample exhibits. By 1948, a room at the Lennox had risen to $3.50 a night. (Courtesy of the Carondelet Historical Society.)

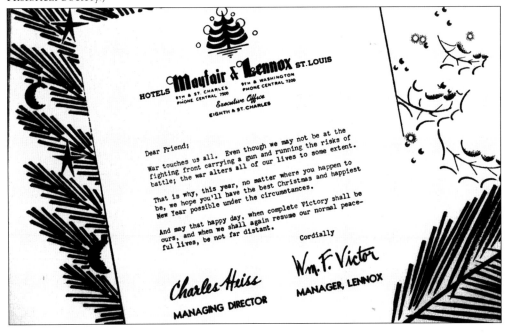

Press Club Daily Edition

All the news that fit to eat

TOP OF THE LENNOX HOTEL – ST. LOUIS, MISSOURI

Spots (SOUPS)

SOUP OF THE DAY (CUP) **95**
Please ask your waitress what's available today

Cup of Steak Soup. ....

Cup of Clam Chowder ....

Newspaper (SALADS)

NEWS EDITOR **1.00**
Tossed house salad with crisp greens and tomato wedge. Choice of dressing.

CITY EDITOR **3.25**
Chef's deluxe salad with crisp greens, Swiss and American cheese, ham, turkey, tomato wedges and hard-boiled eggs. Choice of dressing.

REWRITE COLLAGE . **1.25**
Cheese with peaches, pears or pineapple

ANCHOR MAN **3.95**
Royal fruit plate with pineapple wedge and fresh fruit in season, with cottage cheese

Bulletin (THE BIG MAX)

One of the Press Club's most popular sandwiches is the Big Max. Named after former Club President Max Roby the Big Max is a thick, juicy, delicious hamburger. Roby is a former KSD newsman.

The Big Max is served with french fries, pickle wedge and your choice of cole slaw or lettuce and tomato.

$3.25
With Cheese .25 extra

The Headline (ENTREES)
– Served with French Fries and Vegetable of the Day –

Final Edition (SANDWICHES)
– All Sandwiches Served with Cole Slaw & Garnish –

Bulldog **2.75**
Ham and Swiss cheese on rye.

Five Star **2.75**
Roast beef sandwich, hot or cold.

Filler **3.45**
Rueben sandwich with German potato salad.

The Press Club established its headquarters on the 23rd floor in 1957. A private elevator whisked the organization's 330 members to a central dining room, card rooms, men's bar, and sun deck. Their menu, printed in newspaper lingo, included the Big Max named for Max Roby, former president of the club, former KSD newsman and a hamburger enthusiast. (Courtesy of the St. Louis Public Library, Special Collections.)

This photograph, taken in 1983, shows the detail of the west wall of the Lennox. The canopy extended around the corner and covered the Washington Avenue entrance. In 1962, a newspaper article reported a woman returned two towels and two napkins she took nine years earlier from the hotel. Gordon Heiss, who succeeded his father as owner of the hotel, sold it in 1967 to the Ben Franklin Systems, and the hotel became a motor hotel. It passed through several owners until 1982 when Sorkis Webbe Sr. and Jr. added it to their family of hotels, the Mayfair and the Gateway. The room rate then was about $25 a night. They partnered with Pantheon Corporation, headed by the late Leon Strauss, to convert the Lennox into 100 luxury apartments. After seven years, economic hard times strangled the project. (Courtesy of Landmarks Association of St. Louis; photograph by Mackey and Associates.)

Pantheon left its mark, the 25-story mural on the east wall of the hotel. The company hired New York–based artist Jeffrey Greene, who specializes in a colorful multidimensional art form called trompe l'oeil (trick of the eye) painting. The mural cost about $175,000 and took four months to recreate the elegant terra cotta design of the building's facade facing Washington Avenue. In the meantime, the convention center was built next door to the Lennox, and the city's Land Clearance for Redevelopment Authority took over the Lennox following foreclosure on the hotel's federally insured mortgage. (Courtesy of Mackey Mitchell Associates, architect; photograph by Barbara Elliot Martin.)

This is the restored lobby with the addition of a bar. The filigree brass elevator doors are original, as is the paneling. The hotel now has 165 one-bedroom suites. The adjoining living rooms have sofas, desks, and wet bars. The Rathskeller was not restored and is now a modern restaurant called the Washington Avenue Bistro. (Courtesy of Historic Restoration Properties, Inc.; photograph by Alise O'Brien.)

CONCLUSION

Since its founding in 1764, St. Louis has maintained a fine reputation as a place where hospitality is a way of life. In the beginning, there were simple boarding houses and inns, but by the time of the Civil War and following that tragic period, our hotels grew to greatness. Establishments were created that are today legendary such as the Southern, the Planters' House, the Lindell, and the St. Francis.

As the Louisiana Purchase Exposition developed, a new hotel era started with places such as the Jefferson, the George Washington, and the very first of the many hotels to be built by E. M. Statler, the Inside Inn. The behemoth, frame building was the only hotel actually inside the grounds of St. Louis's 1904 World's Fair. There were a good number of other hotels, large, small, and in between, built to accommodate fairgoers. Many of these structures survive today.

Prior to World War I, a small wave of hotels would be built, such as the Branscome, but the war virtually put a stop to such construction. Then war was over, and we were at the dawn of the Roaring Twenties and the seemingly endless "Coolidge prosperity." Within months following the armistice, the building of new, more modern hotels began again, as we entered the golden era of hotel construction.

This book documents five of the finest hotels in our city's history from this euphoric time and all of them have survived the Great Depression, World War II, the flight to suburbia, multiple owners, closures, and the all-too-real threat of the wrecking ball. These hotels all share a similar exterior of St. Louis–made brick and terra cotta, but each has a different story to tell. Even though most St. Louisans have never stayed under their roofs, most have fond memories of good times spent in the public rooms of these wondrous places. But if this is not the case, just seeing these testaments to a period of plenty is enough to buoy the spirit.

Maybe you or someone in your family was at the grand opening of the Starlight Roof and Zodiac Room of the Chase Hotel in December 1940 and danced to Orrin Tucker's orchestra with Wee Bonnie Baker singing, "Oh Johnny, Oh!" You might have been among the first to enjoy the Mayfair salad dressing or the Welsh Rarebit at the inn's Hofbrau bar. Was that not Van Johnson at a corner table?

You might recall being serenaded by a strolling violinist in the cool, dark-paneled Rathskeller of the Lennox. There was al fresco dining at the Jug patio of the Coronado (for a time simply called the St. Louis Sheraton) and libations in the dark confines of that hotel's basement bar, the Coal Hole. Maybe you met a friend in the lobby of the Statler before seeing the 1944 world premiere of *Meet Me in St. Louis* at the Loew's State Theater across the street.

The memories and stories seem to cling to these great hotels like ivy and, now that these buildings have all been restored, their past seems more alive than ever. These hotels are places of dreams and because of them, many of the dreams came true. And interestingly enough, it is still happening today.

—Ron Elz (Johnny Rabitt)

ACKNOWLEDGMENTS

First I would like to thank Gene Donaldson, my photographer, not only for his skill behind the lens, but also for his steadying influence and constant encouragement.

Thanks to Aldo Martinez of the Coronado for allowing me to use Preston Bradshaw's photos given to him by Judy Miller, Bradshaw's daughter. Thanks to George Cassimates, former Chase maitre d', for sharing his album of stars who appeared at the Chase.

I appreciate, too, the Carondelet Historical Society for lending me Julia King's scrapbook documenting the Mayfair and the Lennox hotels. Thanks, also, to the Landmarks Association of St. Louis, Inc., not only for their research assistance, but also for their continuing efforts to preserve the buildings that mark our heritage.

Thank you to the Mercantile Library at the University of Missouri–St. Louis and the Missouri Historical Society. A special thanks is extended to the St. Louis Public Library Fine Arts and Special Collections Departments for their patient and efficient service.

I would like to thank everyone who contributed photographs and memories that made this book come alive.

My special thanks goes to Julius Hunter for writing the foreword and to Ron Elz for adding the conclusion.

Finally, I acknowledge my mother who instilled in me a curiosity about the past.

BIBLIOGRAPHY

THE STATLER

Architectural Forum, December 1917, January and February 1918.

St. Louis Post-Dispatch, November 14, 1917, November 11, 1917, September 22, 1917. "Story of Inside Inn," June 3, 1952. "Gateway Hotel Fire," November 12, 1990.

St. Louis Star Times. "Widow Finds It Fun to Direct $20,000,000 Statler Hotel Chain," August 5, 1937.

America's Extraordinary Hotelman, Ellsworth Statler's biography, by Floyd Miller.

Be My Guest, by Conrad Hilton and thesis by Cathleen Baird of the Hospitality Industry Archives, University of Houston.

Landmarks Association of St. Louis. "In Danger: The Gateway Hotel," March 18, 2001.

A Bed For The Night, by Rufus Jarman.

St. Louis Globe Democrat. "Want a Job Paying $100 a Week? Be a Bellhop," February 18, 1951.

Preservation Issues. Missouri Department of Natural Resources, March/April 1997.

THE CHASE

St. Louis Globe-Democrat, March 9, 1967, March 28, 1971, and March 11, 1978.

Profile St. Louis, April 12, 1977.

Rivertown Hospitality, by Norbury L. Wayman, 1981.

St. Louis Post-Dispatch, January 30, 1985, and Chase Hotel Advertising Section, March 3, 1985, May 22, 1986. Business Section, September 14, 1989, March 18, 1999.

South Side Journal, January 27, 1986, and January 29, 1986.

St. Louis Business Journal, July 14, 1986.

Southwest City Journal, November 6, 1991.

St. Louis Magazine, March 1998.

"The Legacy Room at the Chase."

Meet Me in the Lobby, by Candace O'Connor.

THE MAYFAIR

St. Louis Globe-Democrat, August 23, 1925, July 24, 1931, September 3, 1961, and March 9, 1983.

The Censor, September 3, 1925.

St. Louis Commerce Magazine, March, 1972.

St. Louis Post-Dispatch, March 9, 1978, January 16, 1983, December 11, 1983, January 22, 1992, March 5, 1996, and August 24, 1997.

St. Louis Construction News, January 17, 1979.

Sidestreets St. Louis, by Mary Costantin, 1981.

Downtowner, February, 1990.

St. Louis Commerce Magazine, May, 1991.

THE CORONADO

Hotel Coronado, 1920s.

St. Louis Globe-Democrat, September 5, 1947, December 7, 1953.

St. Louis Post-Dispatch, October 13, 1968.

Landmarks Letter, March/April and May/June 2004.

THE LENNOX

St. Louis Post-Dispatch, September 1, 1929, March 13, 1985, November 3, 1993, August 2, 1995, Business Section, October 17, 2001.

St. Louis Globe-Democrat, June 1, 1967.

St. Louis Business Journal, April 4, 1983.